The Dangers of Self Idolatry

A Christian Journey from Self Destruction to Salvation

Table of Contents

Forward

This book reflects my personal spiritual journey from being a staunch Atheist to a believing follower of Jesus Christ. This book is entirely truthful in that it shows my struggles, my flaws, and my honest innermost thoughts and ideas; thoughts that others might be able to relate with and share in their own struggle with faith, belief and trust in God, in an increasingly modern and increasingly secular world that wants to pull us further and further away from Him. I wrote this book because I felt called by God to help others have a relationship with Him, in order to overcome their daily fears, worries, and anxieties, and to have more peace and joy in their lives. This calling not only gave me a direction and purpose for my life, but it also literally saved me from the very brink of death.

Chapter 1. Receiving the Sign

"**Maybe what I need to do with my life is to help people overcome fear, but it can only happen through a relationship with God**." I said to my father in his living room, back in 2012, during a very turbulent time of my life. Then suddenly and unexpectedly, and all by itself, the iPhone 4S in the left front pocket of my pants starts to play music. (It never did this before nor has since then, to play music without being prompted to, as it would have taken at least six or seven steps to have gotten through the screen lock and music selection process). When I took the phone out to see what happened, I noticed the song title was "I Saw the Sign". It was an early 1990's pop song I had on my phone. Out of the 864 songs in my phone at the time, it randomly played that particular song at that particular moment, right after I said, "Maybe what I need to do with my life is to help people overcome fear, but it can only happen through a relationship with God." Was this really a sign from God? And if so, what does it mean? This single event redirected the course of my entire life and I guess you can say that, for whatever reason, God literally saved my life.

"Help people overcome fear, but it can only happen through a relationship with God." The reason why this message was so significant was because in my experience, everything else we hold onto for security and fulfillment is impermanent and perishable. From personal experience, I know that money, jobs, marriage, family, friends, social status, youth and beauty, material possessions like houses, cars, clothes, jewelry and "toys", or our reputations, nothing we hold onto is as permanent as we want it to be. Also, fear seems to be the root of so much suffering in the world. Whether it is anxiety, worry, stress, rage, greed, jealousy, selfish ambition, lust, lack of compassion and callousness, conflict and violence...fear, in one form or another, seems to be the root of all of those horrible emotions. Fear of getting hurt, fear of being humiliated or looked down upon, fear of rejection and abandonment fear of getting taken advantage of, fear of not having enough, fear and stress are the origin of so many terrible behaviors.

Up until that moment, I already had a plan of selling everything I owned, getting a one way plane ticket to China, spending all of my money on prostitutes and partying, and then eventually ending my life with a drug overdose. I had already sold all of my stocks and valuable coins, bought the plane ticket from San Francisco to Shanghai, and gotten a travel visa from the Chinese embassy. I was ready to have one final blast before I checked myself out of this world. I had been clinically depressed before during much of my life where I contemplated ending my life and even times when I wished that God would give me a deadly disease, but this was the first time I truly had a plan of burning myself out, and then eventually, fading away. I had previously always been afraid of committing suicide, worried about hurting my parents and ending up in hell, but this time, I was so frustrated and so angry with life that I didn't care anymore about where I might end up. Besides, due to my lack of faith, I didn't really entirely believe in hell anyway.

What precipitated this plan of ending my life was that I was dating a woman whom I was deeply in love with. Everything seemed to be going perfect. I thought I was going to marry her and then we were going to live happily ever after. We moved really fast and even though we'd only been dating for five months, I had already moved in with her after the first month. I had already met her family, especially her father in Taiwan, and she had met my family here. She wanted me to propose to her, and I did, and she said yes. Everything seemed to be on course towards marriage, then a successful life together with good careers, multiple homes, wealth and then children.

Then suddenly, the company that I worked for as a temporary contractor decided not to renew my contract (the position was a well-paying one, and I thought they were going to convert me to become a permanent employee, but instead, they decided to end my six month contract early, without much of an explanation). Following my termination, I lost my confidence, and in my fearful and anxious state, I started an argument with her, which then made her break up with me. I remember that right after it happened, I was actually relieved, because the whole time I was with her, I felt nervous and worried about her possibly breaking up with me as I was always worried about not being good enough for her. When she finally did break up with me, it was almost a relief at first, just to get it over with, because I had expected it to happen anyway, but later, I realize how much I had lost through the breakup. Given that I felt like I lost my one chance for happiness, my one chance for a successful and wonderful life, I wanted to give up everything and end my life, but before that, I was going to have a lot of fun with burning through my life savings with lots of partying, lots of sex, and perhaps, lots of drugs and alcohol.

However, before that happened, God saved me. God told me to redirect my life towards Him, and nothing else. "Help people overcome fear, but it can only happen through a relationship with God." I don't even know why I said that to my father, since it wasn't like I even believed very much in God, in Jesus, or in the miraculous and supernatural things in the Bible, and my father wasn't even a Christian, but for whatever reason, I said it, and then the confirmation from the sign set me on a path towards trying to grow my faith, my trust, my belief in God, and overcoming my own fears through a relationship with Him and trying desperately to help others do the same.

Chapter 2. Starting off Atheist and Challenging God

I didn't start off believing in God. I was actually raised not to believe in anything. In fact, I remember once having a conversation with a Jewish friend in eighth grade where I told him, "I can't imagine living in a world where God exists." As a child and then as an adult, I had always thought that religion was nothing more than a silly, irrational, and unreasonable superstition. I thought God and the Bible were just made up, and mere figments of people's imaginations. I proudly thought I didn't I need to believe in the concept of God, and I thought religion was a crutch for weak people who needed an imaginary friend in order to comfort themselves. I thought I didn't need that like they did because I was "strong" whereas they were weak. I never thought religion should be taken seriously and I always wanted to believe in science, reason, evidence, and proof. One of my favorite childhood idols was Mr. Spock from the Star Trek TV show, since he was cold, unemotional, logical, calculating, intelligent and a little aloof. I loved fantasy novels and science fiction shows as a kid, and that's what I had equated with religion. I thought religion was purely man-made and to be taken as more fantasy than reality. (However, while I was thinking this way, I was also very anxious, very isolated, and always worried about not being good enough). I'd always thought "You'd have to be insane to believe in the crazy stories of the Bible!"

I remember arguing with my Korean American Christian roommate in my first year of college, asking him question after question as to why he believed in the Bible, and not being convinced when he quoted me verse after verse from that book. I wanted him to tell me something outside of the Bible that I could believe in, which might convince me of the validity of what he was telling me about his religion, but he never did. I thought to myself, "How could he be so simple minded and so ignorant of reality? Can't he see that what he believes is silly and scientifically inaccurate?" To me, at that time, the Bible was just another book, nothing more, nothing less. It contained no holiness and I had no special reverence for it. It was just a series of words printed on paper, much like any of the comic books, novels, and non-fiction books I had read during my life. It wasn't until my senior year in college, after I had been exposed to some Christians whom I observed, genuinely seemed more at peace with their lives than I was, and who also seemed a lot nicer than I was, that I seriously thought about converting to Christianity.

I recall one Taiwanese American Christian schoolmate in college who just seemed so at ease, so calm and so happy every time I saw him, even though I didn't think he had reason to be. There was something really odd about his appearance. He was skinny, had lots of facial flaws, his teeth looked uneven, his hair was so thin that he was practically bald, and he wore extremely thick glasses. I remember one of my roommates used to make fun of him, calling him "pinhead", because my roommate thought he looked like a character from the Hellraiser horror movie. This young man almost seemed like he might have been deformed. And yet, he was still so happy. That really surprised me.

When I asked him why he believed in God, he said that he used to be very angry at his father, because his father passed down the physical traits that made him look the way he did. However, after he became a believer, he stopped hating his father, and he had more joy, peace, and love in his life. Later on, I noticed that some others Christians I met were just nice, wholesome people, who

14

enjoyed getting together, sharing meals, singing songs, and gathering together to talk deeply about the Bible and how to be better, more considerate, and happier people. This seemed very different than some of my other friends who, when we got together, there was more "rough talk", more showing off, making fun of others, more alcohol drinking, more interest in sexual behavior, and more superficial interests, such as money, job titles, and purchase of material things. Some of the Christians I met just seemed nicer and happier, overall.

So one day, during my senior year in college, I asked another Taiwanese American Christian friend to sit down with me and to convince me to believe in the Bible. I asked him question after question about miracles, about the resurrection of Christ, about walking on water, about the parting of the Red Sea, and about faith healing...but unfortunately, he didn't have the answers I was hoping for and by the end of the meeting, I still was not convinced of the truth of those parts of the Bible. So I walked away disappointed, unconvinced and unconverted. My belief in science and logic were so strong that there was no room in my mind for anything else other than what scientists had told me to be true and what my own eyes and ears could perceive, and that was, that the miracles of the Bible cannot possibly happen. I also had a hard time in believing in anything that I couldn't understand on my own. I thought that if I couldn't logically comprehend it, then it couldn't possibly be real. I needed a "rational" explanation for everything in order for me to accept it as true.

It wasn't until several years after college that I met some Koreans who were avid church-goers and I dated a Korean Christian woman, that I started attending a small Korean American church in Richmond, CA. I also started attending a Bible study group held by a Korean pastor in Berkeley, and it was then that I really started reading the Bible, especially the New Testament, and I was very impressed by Jesus' teachings on love, forgiveness, and compassion. However, even though I would later get baptized in the pastor's Presbyterian church, and even though I attended church and prayed in front of others, in all honesty, I still had serious doubts about the existence of God, the possibility of miracles, and the existence of an afterlife (both heaven and hell). Every time I prayed, part of me wondered if I was just talking to myself, and when I prayed in front of others, I did it partially for show. I still believed in my own five senses and in my own perception of reality more so than in the Bible and I still had more faith in science and in scientific researchers, than in the concept of God and the Bible.

So, truth-be-told, even though I was a baptized, for many years after, I still didn't really believe in the Bible as much more than a philosophical guide for how to live a better life. When I prayed, I was never sure if God was actually listening to me since I was never sure if God even existed. So in regards to following everything the Bible said about sin, generosity, forgiveness, self-sacrifice, humility, gratitude, faith and belief, I really wasn't very obedient to it, nor did I submit myself to God's will in my life. Generally speaking, I tried not to commit any "big" sins, but for the most part, I didn't really look or act very differently than any average person you might meet on the street, nor did I want to. I didn't want people to think I was a "Jesus freak" or a crazy religious "nut job", out to try to push my views on others. I thought of the teachings of the Bible as a series of suggestions that I could take or leave, rather than a set of commands that I had to bow down to, and obey. I confess now that even though I called myself a Christian, I didn't really take the Bible, or God, very seriously. I really wanted to fit in with the rest of society, rather than stand out and be different from those around me. I was more afraid of society and valued people's opinions, rather than afraid of God, and valuing His.

Therefore, rather than submit to the word of God, I had a tendency of just going with the flow of those around me. What I saw my friends do, what I saw on TV, what I saw in the movies, what I saw on the internet, and what I saw with my peers, I simply followed along, even though it may have gone against what the Bible teaches. I had a bad habit of being proud and glorifying myself, lying, committing sexual immorality, stealing music online, buying counterfeit movies, using vulgar language, disrespecting the name of God, easily losing my temper, and I struggled with lust and pornography ever since I was a child.

It was in this kind of state that I received the sign from God. In my time of real desperation, when I was the closest I had ever gotten towards taking my own life, I had such little faith, and my doubts about God, miracles, and the supernatural far exceeded my belief and my trust in Him. However the miracle of my phone playing a song about seeing a sign (right when I said I should help people have a relationship with God), was just too big of a coincidence for me to dismiss as random chance, mere coincidence or bizarre mechanical malfunction. I chose to believe that God was watching me, that He has always been watching me, and that He cared enough about me to give me a message as to guide my life, and I am grateful that He saved me, that He saved my life. However, even after this miracle, I still had a long way to go in truly believing in everything in the Bible. Throughout this journey, I still struggled with my faith, especially when things got bad in my life.

Chapter 3. Waiting for God, Trying to Overcome My Fears

When I received the sign to help people overcome fear through a relationship with God, I was actually very confused. Prior to that, I had no intention of going into any kind of Christian ministry. At that time, in 2012, I hadn't even stepped inside of a church since my divorce, about two years before. Because of my divorce and how my church had gotten involved with trying to "fix" our marriage (but actually made it worse), I actually had a really negative image of church, and I had a really hard time even trusting churches and trusting other Christians. I didn't think the Christians at my church were very compassionate or understanding of my pain and my struggle during my divorce. During my divorce, amongst my Christian brothers and sisters, I found judgement, but not a lot of understanding, or a desire to connect, heal, or help to carry my painful burden of a breaking marriage and a breaking life. I experienced so much fear and conflict in my marriage, and then even more fear and distrust from members of my own church. And now, God wanted me to help people have a relationship with Him? It made no sense to me at all.

Frankly, at that moment, I wasn't even sure if I believed that God existed at all. How was supposed to go out and evangelize something that I didn't truly believe in? Also, I thought I was the least credible person to do any kind of ministry. I was insecure, prone to anxiety, had a short temper, and was vulnerable to bouts of depression. Why in the world would God want ME to spread His message? I really didn't make any sense. Besides, with all my problems, and my troubled past, I seemed like the LAST person to talk to people about God. Who on earth would believe ME?

However, I also felt that if this really was a sign from God, then I need to take it seriously. All I could think about was God and how to overcome fear. So I started attending a church again. I went to an Episcopalian church (because I was a big fan of Episcopalian author Marcus Borg) near my home in the Oakland hills and I attended that church for about 3 years. Eventually, I even went to and Episcopal seminary at the Graduate Theological Union in Berkeley, California to see if I might somehow become more interested in becoming a minister. Unfortunately, it didn't happen, and after getting sick into my second semester, I decided to drop out. During this whole period of time, I kept asking God to give me more signs and to guide my path. I never got a sign that was as clear as what I got in my father's living room, but I tried to interpret whatever I could and to be obedient to God's will. I also tried to face and overcome my fears, and therefore, become less prone to having anxiety attacks, stressing out, losing my temper, and feeling anxious and nervous all the time.

I tried very hard to step outside of my comfort zone in order to overcome my fears by exposing myself to them. I went to an almost all Caucasian church where I was often the only person of color (I'm Chinese American). I traveled to Italy by myself, then to the American Deep South alone. I wrote a blog where I talked about experiences of facing my fears, and I also exposed my personal life to the public by blogging about it. I went bungee jumping and sky diving, and like I wrote earlier, I went to seminary to see if it might spark an interest to become a minister (which it didn't). I signed up to be a driver for Lyft (a smartphone rider-sharing service), where I drove over 8,000 strangers of all different races, social status, and sexual orientations from all over the world, and would sometimes have very deep and intimate conversations with them. During the whole time, I tried to tell myself not to be afraid or to overreact because God was watching me, and that God wanted me to overcome my own fears and help others do the same. Over time, I learned not to overreact as much as before. My flight or fight response started to dissipate more and more.

However, even after all of these experiences, my faith in God didn't really grow very much. I was less fearful than before, but my faith and belief stayed the same. The denomination of church that I attended, the Episcopal Church, tended not to believe in the Bible literally, and thus, its members interpret the Bible so that belief in the supernatural wasn't necessary to being a member. The Episcopal Church stressed "reason" as one of its most important tenants, and therefore, it tended not to focus on the Bible as much, but instead, focused on human logic and rationality. They tended to also focus much more on political and social justice issues, things here and now, rather than on matters of faith, belief in Jesus, in supernatural miracles or in the afterlife.

This train of thought went pretty well with my spiritual state at the time since I believed more in myself and in humanity than I did in God. I still had a lot of pride, a big ego, and I had a lot of confidence in myself, in humans, in science, in money, in other man-made and material things, and I believed in my five senses more so than in supernatural occurrences or things beyond my own understanding or the understanding of humanity. When I attended the Episcopal Church and attended the Episcopal Seminary, I was still a very proud and a very ambitious person, and I believe it was this pride and ambition that **prevented** me from having stronger faith in a limitless and omnipotent God. God requires us to bow down to Him and to confess our own very limited, very ignorant and very sinful nature, while acknowledging His very UNLIMITED, very omniscient, and very perfect nature. Without this mindset, it's hard to actually engage in real worship, since worship requires us to look UP to an infinitely good, infinitely powerful, and sometimes very mysterious God, not look face to face at a limited "god", which can only do things that human beings can explain and comprehend.

Chapter 4. Learning to be Humble, Having More Faith

I eventually left the Episcopal Church and then went to another more evangelical, but still very liberal church in Oakland, California. When I was talking to the pastor about the subject of humility, he recommended a book to me called, "Humility", by a South African minister named Andrew Murray, written over a hundred years ago. Reading this short fifty-four page book changed my whole perspective on faith and on belief in the nature of God, in Jesus, in the Bible, and in supernatural miracles. Even though I thought I had received a sign from God several years before, which saved my life, I was still extremely skeptical about things that were beyond my understanding, and there were lots of times when I even questioned the validity of the sign as a real message from God or not. I still didn't believe in miracles, in supernatural forces, or on things that science couldn't prove by "rational" and "reasonable" means. I still thought "seeing is believing".

Even though a part of me thought that I received a sign from God to go into ministry, another part of me thought that maybe it was just some big coincidence, some malfunction of my phone, or maybe even that there was someone at Apple Computers was eavesdropping on my conversation with my father and controlling my phone so that it would play the right song at the right moment. I was still looking for some kind of "rational" explanation, any kind of explanation, that didn't have anything to do with the supernatural, or with things I couldn't wrap my head around (I really didn't want people to think I was some "crazy religious Jesus freak"). I wanted to know what was happening and I wanted to be the one in control, the one who could predict everything, and the one who had all the answers. And I think it was this prideful attitude in my life which prevented me from having stronger faith in God. My faith was in myself and in mankind, not in God.

However, after reading the Humility book, I realized that what prevented me from having more faith in God and in the Bible was my own pride, ego, arrogance, self-exalting, and self-glorifying nature. The main premise of that book is that you can't have faith without humility. So, even if you have a PhD or Master's Degree in Theology, but if you're still arrogant, prideful, self-righteous, egotistical, narcissistic, conceited or vain, then all you'll have is academic knowledge of religion and the Bible, but you won't actually have real faith.

The author, Andrew Murray, says, "Humility and faith are more nearly allied in Scripture than many know. See it in the life of Christ. There are two cases which He spoke of a great faith." (page 37, Humility) The author referenced people that Jesus proclaimed to have great faith when they humbled themselves before him, after requesting that Jesus heal their servant and their family member. Specifically, he was talking about the Roman centurion, in Matthew 8:5-13, who wanted Jesus to heal his sick servant. The centurion was someone with status and power, but he humbled himself before Jesus by saying that 8 *"Lord, I do not deserve to have you come under my roof. But just say the word, and my servant will be healed.* 9 *For, I myself am a man under authority, with soldiers under me. I tell this one, 'Go,' and he goes; and that one, 'Come,' and he comes. I say to my servant, 'Do this,' and he does it."*10 ***And Jesus was amazed at his great faith, "Truly I tell you, I have not found anyone in Israel with such great faith***." Andrew Murray also referred to the Canaanite woman, in Matthew 15:21-28, who pleaded with Jesus to heal her demon-possessed daughter, but whom Jesus rejected and even referred to her people as "dogs", because Jesus' goal was to help the lost children of Israel, not gentiles. But rather than feel insulted and angry, the woman humbled herself even further by acknowledging her status as a dog, and that she was still willing to feed off of the "crumbs that fall from their master's table." 28 *Jesus then responded "Woman, you have great faith! Your request is granted."* Once again, it was her humility that saved her daughter.

I am also reminded of the story of the prodigal son (Luke 15:11-32), who was forced by the consequences of his foolish decisions to be humbled, poor and desperate enough to get a job as a swine herder (something totally abhorrent to Jews) because he was so utterly wretched and hungry. It was in this humbled state that he finally came to his senses, and decided to go back to his father, confess his guilt to God and to his father and then repent.

"14 *After he had spent everything, there was a severe famine in that whole country, and he began to be in need. 15 So he went and hired himself out to a citizen of that country, who sent him to his fields to feed pigs. 16 He longed to fill his stomach with the pods that the pigs were eating, but no one gave him anything. 17 "When he came to his senses, he said, 'How many of my father's hired servants have food to spare, and here I am starving to death! 18 I will set out and go back to my father and say to him: Father, I have sinned against heaven and against you. 19 I am no longer worthy to be called your son; make me like one of your hired servants.' 20 So he got up and went to his father.*" If it wasn't for him being in his hungry, humiliated, dejected, and wretched state, I don't think he would have ever come to his senses to go back to his father to repent.

And then there's the sinful woman, in Luke 7:36-50, who acknowledged her own sinfulness, approached Jesus, got down on her hands and knees, to kiss and pour perfume on his feet, wet them with her tears, and then used her own hair to wash and wipe them. "38 *As she stood behind him at his feet weeping, she began to wet his feet with her tears. Then she wiped them with her hair, kissed them and poured perfume on them*". It was in her humbled, lowly and penitent position that Jesus felt great compassion and mercy for her and forgave her many sins. Thus, I believe that when we humble ourselves before God, and show that we are truly sorry, confess our sins, and make a deep commitment to repent, God shows mercy upon us, and embrace us as His children, reconciling us to Him as He works to heal our broken souls. I know that when I pray in this position and in a state of humility, I can feel God's mercy far more than any other position. There were many times when I poured out my heart to God in this position, and I also wept like the sinful woman, and was afterwards cleansed and healed of my pain and my sin.

And lastly, Jesus's preaching the sermon on the mount of the Beatitudes on Matthew 5:3-10 is full of emphasis on humble submission and repentance before God:

> *"3 Blessed are the poor in spirit, for theirs is the kingdom of heaven.*
>
> *4 Blessed are those who mourn, for they will be comforted.*
>
> *5 Blessed are the meek, for they will inherit the earth.*
>
> *6 Blessed are those who hunger and thirst for righteousness, for they will be filled.*
>
> *7 Blessed are the merciful, for they will be shown*

mercy.

8 Blessed are the pure in heart, for they will see God.

9 Blessed are the peacemakers, for they will be called
children of God.

10 Blessed are those who are persecuted because of
righteousness, for theirs is the kingdom of heaven."

According to the Beatitudes, it's not the proud, arrogant, self-ambitious, self-righteous, and defiant who are blessed, but those who humble themselves before God, who acknowledge their sinful nature, and who have a deep desire to reconcile with the Heavenly Father and who seek peace, mercy and purity of heart.

It was in reading the book, Humility, and then thinking about how often the concept of humility, meekness, gratitude, submission, repentance, and obedience comes up in the Bible again and again, both in the Old Testament and the New Testament, that I started to change the way I prayed, changed the way I thought about my relationship with God, and even changed the way I believed about the Bible, and about the rest of the world. I re-assessed my role in the Universe as tiny and almost completely insignificant, while thinking of the role of God as infinitely large, infinitely wise, infinitely powerful, and infinitely good and holy. It was then that I realized that all along, I was supposed to have feared and humbly respected, worshipped and obeyed God, rather than fearing, and respecting humanity and human made concepts, like power, status, and money.

When I pray now, I regularly bow down on my hands and knees, prostrate, with my head touching the floor. I thank God for all that He's blessed me with (good health, abundant food, shelter, abundant warm clothing, family, friends, the Bible, his son Jesus Christ who died to save me, a job, financial security, freedom, good weather, clean running drinking water, flush toilets, hot showers, protection from danger, etc.), and I would ask that God helps to humble all of us, for all of us to worship Him, and to heal the brokenness in my family, and in the entire world.

In the past, I used to pray to ask God to give me the things that my friends had, or things that my peers and society says I should have because I was self-ambitious, arrogant, and dissatisfied with my life. I compared myself to people on TV, with people in movies, with my wealthier friends and wealthier people in society, and I would ask God to give me what those people had. I thought of my relationship with God almost as one between equals, rather than that of a humble slave towards a sovereign king. Back then, I didn't think I needed to respect God and submit to his authority. I thought I would only follow the parts of the Bible that I wanted to follow, rather than try to be obedient to the whole thing. I was presumptuous to think that I had a special relationship with God, that we were "pals" and that He knew of my struggles, and therefore I didn't need to take Him that seriously and obey all of His commands.

But now, when get down on the floor to pray on my hands and knees, I would sometimes start crying, and even start sobbing, like a baby. In this position, much like that of the sinful woman, in Luke 7:36-50, who washed Jesus' feet with her tears, sometimes the emotions that would come out would be so intense and the memories from the past, so strong, that I couldn't help but to weep like a child. All the pain, all the frustration, all the anger, all the feelings of injustice and unfairness, all the sadness and loss, all the bitterness...would be washed away with those tears and released in those sobs. And in those moments, I knew that God was with me, overseeing my humble submission, seeing my desire to reconcile with Him, and He would show me mercy to me because I acknowledge that I'm a sinful person, deserving punishment, and that my greatest desire is to be released from my sin and to be reconciled with Him. It was wonderful to experience each of these cleansing and healing moments.

As I made more and more of an effort to humble myself in worshipping God and to submit to His will, rather than my own, I noticed changes started happening in my life. Every day, several times a day, I would pray like this, thanking God for all of His generosity, and to also to heal me of my brokenness. And in his mercy and omnipotence, and with the new found belief that God is capable of doing all things, I called out to God to cure me of a lustful addiction that I had struggled with for most of my life, since I was ten years old. I asked God to give me Alzheimer's for all of my lustful memories of pornography and sexual immorality so that I would forget the sexually filthy things I've seen and done in my life. I had been in bondage to this addiction most of my life, but since earnestly and humbly praying to God for help in cleansing my mind and my spirit, God has cured me to never engage in that behavior again. This has been a real miracle because I tried many times to stop with my own will, but I failed every time. However, this time, with the belief that God is merciful and that God is truly unlimited in His power, He was able to give me the strength to overcome my addiction. It was not my own will power that overcame this because I already tried and failed many times on my own, but it was God's power which cleansed my mind, and gave me the strength to be released from its bondage. Now, I'm not saying that God will always give us what we ask for. For His own reasons, God may decide not to give us what we ask for (maybe for our own protection, maybe because He thinks we aren't ready for it, or maybe to humble us), but **I now acknowledge that there is no limit to what God can do, if He chooses to do it because His power truly is unlimited**.

The Bible is actually full of parts that talk about our need for humility and to humble and submit ourselves to God, and how God loves the humble, the obedient and the penitent, but despises the proud, the disobedient, and the un-repentant (such as Proverbs 3:34 *He mocks proud mockers but shows favor to the humble and oppressed*). As I continued to meditate on humility, and to humbly and gratefully pray every day, I started to realize just how arrogant, prideful, egotistical, self-aggrandizing, self-glorifying, and self-centered I have always lived, during my entire life. I started to diminish my sense of self-importance and self-centeredness in the universe and my desire to project to the world a "perfect" and "successful" image, and I tried to be more honest about who I am, what I'm really capable of, and what I've really been through, rather than maintain a false image, a lifelong performance of the person I wanted people to think I am. This whole time, God gave me the courage to be who I really am, rather than pretend to be the person other people wanted me to be. **I started to see how great and how grand God is, and how extremely insignificant, limited, sinful and flawed I have always been**.

Chapter 5. Believing in the "Impossible"

As I said earlier, coming from a "logical" and "rational" Atheist background, I had a really hard time believing in the entirety of the Bible. That is, I had a hard time believing in an unlimited and omnipotent God, and believing in supernatural concepts like Jesus' resurrection, miracle healings, or walking on water. I had a hard time believing that God could literally do ANYTHING and EVERYTHING, even things I couldn't understand and comprehend. It all just seemed too far-fetched, fantastic, unprovable and unscientific to me. I asked myself, where is God? I don't see Him, hear Him, and I can't touch Him. I had far more faith in my own five senses and in the "truth" of science and the scientific method, and based on such a method, I knew for certain that the supernatural miracles of the Bible could not happen. Even though I had considered myself to be Christian for almost two decades, and had even briefly gone to seminary to study Christianity, ever since the beginning, I was still very skeptical and I still had a really hard time with belief in God.

However, one day, while having a theological conversation with a conservative pastor friend of mine, he asked me if I believed that Christ was resurrected from the dead. My honest response was, "I'm not sure". Based on my knowledge of science and medicine, I really wasn't sure if I could believe that a person could be scourged, crucified, killed and stabbed in the chest, and three days later be returned to life, walk around, talk to people, and finally, ascend to heaven. I still had some serious doubts about it. My friend then told me that based on what he knows of the Bible, I wasn't a Christian. I wasn't saved. He said that since one of the most important aspects of being a Christian is in believing in Jesus' resurrection, I didn't qualify since I didn't believe in Jesus' resurrection. This whole time, I thought I could be a Christian in my philosophy, but not in my belief.

When he told me this, initially, I was a little offended. How could he say this about me? After all, I've been baptized, I had gone to church for years, and I had even attended seminary! I had read the Bible multiple times, and I prayed regularly. But still, a part of me knew he was right, and somehow, someway, I needed to believe in what I considered to be impossible. It all came back to how I could believe in things in the Bible that I didn't want to believe because it contradicted so much of what I already believed to be true (ie, science says that miracles cannot happen in real life). That conversation I had with my Taiwanese American friend back in my senior year of college whom I asked question after question about miracles, finally had to be addressed. I had to believe.

But reading the book, Humility, by Andrew Murray really changed my faith life. Given that I now understood that humility and faith are deeply intertwined, **I started to wonder if humility and BELIEF are also be connected as well**? In other words, is my lack of belief in miracles due to my own pride and my own arrogance in thinking that I already knew everything about the universe, the laws of nature, and the nature of God? I asked myself if I can truly trust my five senses in determining what is reality in the universe, and also, can I truly trust science in being able to always predict and control everything. Also, had I compartmentalized God into a figure that I could easily understand and relate to? Did I make God in my own image?

My entire life, I've been taught in school, by my family, by my friends, and by my society that I should trust in science and in scientists. I was told that I needed to trust researchers, and that I needed to trust evidence, proof, logic and reason. I was taught not to trust in the irrational, the unreasonable and the "crazy". You know, just like the stuff that's portrayed in parts of the Bible. (ie, the walls of Jericho collapsing by blowing trumpets, Joshua 6:1-27, God killing the firstborn of Egypt, but sparing the Israelites, Exodus 11:1-12:30, God parting the Red Sea, Exodus 13:17-Exodus 14:29, Jesus walking on water, Matthew 14:2-23, Jesus healing a blind man, John 9:6-7). I was told not to have blind faith in anything and that I need to trust sound and rational scientific reasoning and conclusions about the reality of our universe. And generally speaking, that scientific reasoning says that God doesn't exist, that science is the definitive authority on the reality of the world, and that science trumps the Bible, every single time.

However, having gone to public schools and also to college, I know a little bit about how the scientific method works. It's a system that's based on creating a hypothesis, which is then verified or refuted by experimentation and observation. Based on the evidence, the hypothesis is either proved or disproved and a scientific theory is created. So for example, the scientific theory of gravity says that on earth, objects will always fall and accelerate at a rate of 9.8 meters per second (if unhindered by air or liquid resistance). At the same time, science states that in water's liquid state, it is always too viscous (not thick or dense enough) to allow a man to walk on it, on earth, without sinking down below. Assuming these things to always be true about gravity and the viscosity of water, then it's safe to assume that Jesus could not have walked on water, as he would have fallen through the surface. Therefore, that miracle in the Bible is either a lie, an error, or meant to be interpreted as a metaphor, not to be taken literally (I believe this is how many Christians in America today think about miracles in the Bible). The problem with this is that when we don't take the Bible very seriously anymore because we don't believe in the validity and accuracy of it, then we also start to dismiss the validity and seriousness of other parts of the Bible as well. When we don't take the Bible seriously, then it's also easy not to take the morality that's taught in the Bible very seriously, as well.

Therefore, the parts of the Bible where God tells us not to be greedy, not to be self-centered, not to be jealous of what others have, not to be proud, arrogant, entitled and self-glorifying, not to lie, not to steal, not to have sex outside of marriage, not to neglect the needs and suffering of others, not to abuse people, not to disrespect our elders and also, where the Bible tells us to always thank God for all of our blessings, where it tells us to love and forgive one another, even our worst enemies, where it tells us to be humble, where it tells us to be merciful, where it tells us to be compassionate, where it tells us to be self-controlled and not prone to having short tempers and raging behavior, where it tells us to be generous and self-sacrificing, where it tells us to humble ourselves and repent of our sins, where it tells us to worship, exalt and glorify God and God alone, where it tells us to believe in the power of Jesus and of God, when we don't take parts of the Bible seriously anymore because we think we can dismiss them as irrational, illogical, unreasonable, inaccurate, and "crazy", then we end up with people who no longer have faith in God, and what He wants us to do, how He wants us to think and how He wants us to live.

We end up with people who are more focused on exalting, glorifying and praising their own self-image and following their own sense of morality rather than exalting, glorifying and praising God for all his generous blessings, and following the and obeying God's instructions to create a peaceful, harmonious, righteousness and just world. This way of life is not only dangerous for society, but also dangerous for the individual as well. Spending one's life on the worship of one's own self-image is dangerous due to the impermanent and perishable nature of that self-image, and not being obedient to God's will in regards to how we treat others can make us irresponsible, morally bankrupt, and disciples of evil, rather than of good.

So how do I believe in God, in Jesus' resurrection, and in the miraculous and supernatural nature of the Bible, when I've been taught my whole life to only to believe in the "rational", the "reasonable", the "logical", the "scientific", and the "sane"? Reading the Andrew Murray's Humility book, reminded me that I'm not such a "big" person after all, that I'm not the center of the universe, that I'm not the one in control, and I'm not the one who knows everything and can predict everything. I reminded myself to be humble and to thank God for everything in my life and especially, for saving my life through that miraculous sign that I received several years ago and for curing me of my lustful addiction. In other words, I tried to remind myself that I'm not God.

Going with this line of thinking, I then asked myself, "**Do I really know as much about the universe as I think I do? Do I really know as much about reality as much as I think I do**?" All these years, I had accepted the scientific premise that miracles like walking on water are simply impossible, and that you'd have to be a fool, an idiot, or simply crazy to believe in them. They're completely unreasonable. However, for the first time in my life, I started to challenge this belief and I even started to challenge science. I remember from my high school science classes how the scientific method was used to create theories. The basis of the theories has always been experimentation and observations. However, I also know that the concept of God is limitless and infinite. In theory, there is no end to God's power, God's knowledge, God's wisdom, and God's omniscience. **Therefore, I understood that while God has no limitations, humans and humanity does, and science, which is a man-made concept, actually has TREMENDOUS limitations**.

For example, I know that the scientific method is based on experimentation, but that experimentation is ALWAYS limited in scope. In other words, even something as basic as force of gravity, something that everyone on earth can agree exists, is not actually as definitive as most of us thinks it is. This is because the scientific method is always based on experimentation and observation. And I don't care which physicist you are, there is no physicist on earth who will claim that humans have observed EVERY single instance where the force of gravity has acted on earth, let alone in the entire universe.

Estimated Scope of the Entire Universe

Based on a 2016 article in Science, deep field images from the Hubble space telescope estimates that there are **two TRILLION galaxies in the universe**. And based on estimates by physicists at the University of Nottingham in the United Kingdom, it's assumed that there are **100 million stars in each galaxy**. That means that there are an estimated **200,000,000,000,000,000,000** stars in the universe (roughly). And this doesn't include planets, moons, asteroids, or gaseous nebulas. If we ask ourselves how many times that the force of gravity has acted on our planet Earth (ie, a rocks falling to the ground, raindrops falling from the sky, birds landing on a tree branch, a car rolling down the hill), and we multiply that number by 200,000,000,000,000,000,000, then we can assume that the number of times that gravity has occurred in the entire universe is just far too great to count.

In other words, it's simply impossible to capture ALL of reality using the scientific method. Even if a scientist says that they've done one trillion experiments on gravity, or even one trillion times one trillion experiments on gravity, they still cannot say that they have captured, or are able to capture, every single instance of gravity acting in all of reality. **In other words, science ALWAYS takes a smaller sample size of reality, and then extrapolates that sample size to assume that the same is true for the rest of the universe**.

It's kind of like trying to determine the percentage of people of the United States of America who like vanilla or chocolate ice cream. There are currently about 320 million people living in the USA. However, because it would too expensive and maybe too time consuming to survey every single one of the 320 million Americans, researchers might ask just 50,000 Americans, which ice cream flavor they would prefer. And based on the results of that survey, the researchers would claim that they have the correct answer.

However, that result would never be completely accurate because without asking every single one of the 320 million Americans, there's always the possibility of error because by making the assumption that the preference of the 50,000 American sample size completely and accurately reflects the ice cream preferences of all 320 million Americans. And the truth is that this is never the case. The only way to get a completely accurate number is by asking **ALL** 320 million Americans. While you might be able to get a good estimate or a good guess by getting the results of the smaller 50,000 sample size, you will never get a completely precise result. In addition, **there is also the possibility of getting false or inaccurate data from the sample size** (ie, people might lie or change their minds about their ice cream preferences).

We saw a clear example of this in the 2016 presidential election when Hilary Clinton ran against Donald Trump. Based on all the polls, most people assumed that Hilary Clinton was going to win the election. However, when the actual election results came in the next day on Wednesday, November 9th, Trump was found to be the winner. How could the surveys have been so wrong? Why weren't they able to predict the winner of the election? It was because respondents either lied about who they were actually going to vote for (inaccurate data), or the respondent sample size that the researchers polled did not accurately capture all of the preferences of the people who actually voted. Either way, the researchers and surveyors weren't able to accurately predict the results of the election, and almost everyone was shocked by the results of the election in 2016, President Donald Trump. I suspect that for Trump supporters, this victory was a real miracle.

So based on this premise that science is not always as infallible or as invulnerable as I had previously thought, I had to also humble my evaluation of my own knowledge and the knowledge of all of humanity. In other words, **I had to admit to myself that I don't know everything, and that not even all of humanity knows everything about the universe, and about all of reality**. **The scientific method is always based on what's**

observable, but what humans can observe is ALWAYS extremely limited.

It would be like looking at a red apple, and then assuming that based on the red skin color on the outside of the apple, that the entire apple must also be red, from the skin all the way to the apple core. As human beings, this is how we observe the universe. We have an extremely narrow perspective of reality, even with all of our tools and our instruments to capture sight, sound, force, movement, electromagnetic waves, radiation, etc. Therefore, we cannot assume that we already know everything there is to know, not even about whether or not it's possible for a man named Jesus to walk on water, two thousand years ago, or whether or not it's possible for Jesus to die, and then be brought back to life. If I can acknowledge that there are things in the universe that I still don't know, and that there are forces at work that I still cannot fathom, then I have to admit that Jesus walking on water or Jesus being resurrected are indeed possible, and that in fact, all things are possible with God.

If I am truly to humble myself, acknowledge my own extremely limited and ignorant nature, the extremely limited and ignorant nature of all of science and all of humanity, and to acknowledge the grandness and infiniteness of the nature of God, then I have to submit that all the miracles, all the supernatural elements, and all the "unbelievable" parts of the Bible are at least, possible, and that science could have been wrong all these years in dismissing the unexplainable and incomprehensible as "myth" and fantasy. At this point, my belief in the supernatural elements of the Bible now became a choice, whereas previously, I had always assumed that the "rational", "reasonable", and "logical" perspective of science was self-evident, and therefore, I felt compelled to disbelieve in the Bible, and see it as nothing more than a book on moral teachings, but not a book on belief in the omnipotent, omniscient and supernatural God.

Now, don't get me wrong. I'm not trying to completely debunk science and say that gravity doesn't exist and that you'll just float away into space when you step out of your front door, or that you shouldn't see a doctor if you feel chest pains because you don't believe the doctors can help you with an MRI or the right kind of mediation or surgery. Humanity certainly has done a lot to progress our knowledge of the universe and of medicine through scientific research. **However, what I'm saying is that science does not, and cannot ever explain everything about the nature of reality in the universe. And therefore, the decision to believe in God is now a**

free choice, rather than a given that science will always trump God.

In other words, there are still so many things that humans still cannot measure and predict, but that are still in existence. I'm sure that five hundred years ago, no one could fathom the existence of microwaves, nuclear fission, the ability of humans to fly or travel to space. However, that doesn't mean that those things didn't exist or weren't possible. It just meant that five hundred years ago, people weren't able to detect or understand those concepts. I believe that we are in a similar state now and will forever be in such a state. That is, as limited human beings, in our pride and arrogance, as much as we like to tell ourselves that we can know everything about the nature of reality, it is only our big egos which says that and reality dictates that we don't know everything, and that we will never know everything. **We will always be limited in our ability**

to observe and predict the universe. In that way, even though many of us want to deny it, we will never play the role of God in knowing, controlling and predicting everything.

So now, when I read the Bible and I come to a part that seems miraculous, supernatural or unbelievable, I have to remind myself to check my thoughts and say, "Humble yourself, Tony. You don't know as much as you think you do. You don't know for sure that this cannot happen." and I read with a more open mind, whereas I used to immediately dismiss those parts as pure fantasy, myth, or symbolic, and thus, not to be taken seriously. When I read the Bible now, and when I think about the unlimited and all powerful nature of God and the teachings of Jesus, I take them all a lot more seriously than I ever did before. **I now choose to believe that God is capable of literally anything. His power is unlimited and**

his wisdom and knowledge are also unlimited. If God chooses to, he can move mountains, cure diseases, bring dead people back to life, or choose to strike people down in His wrath. However, just because God CAN do anything doesn't always mean that He CHOOSES to do what we want Him to do. God is still the sovereign king over us, and we are His humble slaves. That means that He can choose to do whatever miracles He wishes, and if He doesn't choose to do them, then He doesn't have to. Ultimately, His will is greater than ours, and his plan is greater than ours. We have to humbly submit to Him, and always and continuously be grateful for His rich blessings and praise His holy name, as the source of everything in our lives.

In addition, when I think back on how "rational", "reasonable" and "logical" I used to be, I'm mindful of how those words are often used to describe self-serving behavior as well. When I studied Economics in college, we always made the assumption that human beings are "rational". This means that in economics, we always assume that people try to maximize their own happiness by the way they sell, and by the way they spend. Self-interest, self-preservation, and the profit motive seem to be the most "reasonable" and the most "sane" things to do in life. People behaving in a way that benefits themselves the most seem to be very normal and very reasonable. Yet, how then do we explain the self-sacrificing kind of behavior that Jesus committed when he died as a sacrificial Passover lamb so that we would be saved from God's justice and wrath? How can we explain the level of self-sacrifice that Jesus calls upon his followers to engage in? How can you ask people to give up their own sense of security and their own resources for the sake of glorifying God and helping others who are in need? It seems neither reasonable nor sane, but we all know it's the right thing to do.

Therefore, this is another argument for why I chose to deprioritize reason, in favor of faith, and obedience to God. Jesus calls us to love others **UNREASONABLY**, just like God wanted his faithful and righteous servant Job to also love Him unreasonably as well. Job still praised and loved God, even though there was no longer a reason to, given that God had allowed him to suffer so much. Job loved God for no other reason than because he felt like he had to.

In fact, it would seem like if I had a reason to love someone (ie, they give me money, they give me status, they give me power), then it wouldn't be real love. It would be a transaction. Real love is unconditional, and thus, it's also unreasonable. Heaven forbid if we have to have reasons for loving our own children, and to stop loving them if they happened to fail in living up to those reasons. In the case of real love, we have to love without reason, and without condition. Real love is radical and crazy, because it doesn't have any bounds. We love because Jesus tells us to love, and we humbly submit and obey that command, like non-violent soldiers, without question, and without reason.

I now know that God is the creator of the universe, regardless of whether you believe in Him creating it in 6 days or in the Big Bang theory and evolution. I know that God has played a role in everything in the universe from the very beginning until the end of time. And therefore, when I humbly pray to Him and give Him thanks, I praise Him and glorify His name. In fact, on a daily basis, I repeat the phrase "Thank You Lord" again and again in my thoughts. I do this sometimes several hundred or several thousands of times a day, to remind myself always that God has blessed me with so much in my life, good health, peace, safety, freedom, protection, my family, my friends, financial stability, shelter, warm clothes, the Bible, my job, and for saving my life, Jesus Christ who has given me salvation at the price of his own perfect life …the abundant blessings that God has blessed me with are just too many to count. Being a sinner, I certainly don't deserve any of them. In fact, I deserve God's justice, his wrath, eternal torment in hell, but instead, He has gifted me with all these abundant blessings and with salvation in heavenly paradise after I die, not because of what I've done to deserve it, but because of His great love for me and His great generosity towards all His children, and all I had to do was to bow down and humble myself to Him, confess my sins, turn my life around and repent, and to believe and trust in Him.

Chapter 6. Fear, the Root of Many Evils

Fear, it's that uncomfortable feeling of uneasiness, vulnerability, and distrust that comes from the anticipation or expectation of possible pain. It could be the anticipation of physical pain (like falling and breaking your legs, freezing in cold weather, being burned, drowning in the ocean, or being physically attacked or physically punished), or it could be emotional pain (like rejection, neglect, invalidation, humiliation, denigration, ostracism, isolation, loneliness, abandonment, loss of control, facing the unknown, being bullied or cornered). Thus, the more we anticipate pain, the more frightened and anxious we become. This is why children don't experience as much fear as adults, because children haven't yet experienced as much pain. Once they experience more pain or more trauma, and if they have a strong memory of that painful experience, then they become more fearful and anxious as their anticipation of pain increases. Thus, people who were traumatized a lot, who have strong memories of painful events, who have strong imaginations of possible dangers, or who ruminate a lot about their painful past have a tendency to constantly anticipate pain, and therefore, are constantly fearful and anxious.

The anticipation of pain is also caused by feelings of scarcity of something seemingly crucial. These seemingly crucial things could be a lack of comfort, lack of food, lack of safety, lack of rest, lack of strength, lack of security, lack of time, lack of space, lack of freedom, lack of power, lack of skill, lack of attention, lack of validation, lack of respect, lack of status, lack of money, lack of education level, lack of achievements, lack of "trophies", etc. In not having enough of these seemingly crucial things, the person would then anticipate pain, either physical, or emotional.

When people feel like they are in a mode of scarcity, inadequacy, or poverty of those "crucial" things (whether they truly are or not), their fight, flight or freeze reflex kicks in, as their fear makes them anticipate pain. Therefore, they'll either get angry enough to fight the threat (the perceived cause of the scarcity), panic and run away to escape, or freeze and do nothing, hoping that the fearful thing goes away.

Fear and stress cause so many dysfunctional behaviors in the world. For example, if a young man feels like his manhood has been insulted, this could trigger a fight response, and he might get angry and feel the need to prove his manliness by destroying that which is diminishing his image of himself as a man. When the problems of life seem too overwhelming, and some people feel inadequate and incapable to deal with them, they could decide to escape through drugs, alcohol, gambling, pornography, binge watching TV, social media, work, or they may simply abandon overwhelming situation. And sometimes, if there is chaos or even violence in a home, some members of the family may simply freeze and do nothing as a way of protecting themselves, hoping they be left alone in safety, rather than confront and resolve the cause of the chaos.

Fear and the worry of others taking away our sense of security and sense of control is usually the trigger for anger, hatred and even violence. Fear of never having enough money or other "crucial" resources is the cause of greed and jealousy. Fear of being humiliated, denigrated, insulted, diminished, ignored, neglected, abandoned, and humbled can cause someone to act much more aggressively and callously in order to assert themselves, to get noticed, to compete for dominance and conquest, or to simply to "get even". Fear of being threatened by outsiders can make people act very hostile and defensively (this is what wartime propaganda does, demonizing the enemy, and thus, making them less sympathetic and easier to hurt).

The understanding of the anticipation or fear of physical pain is pretty self-evident. We all know how unsettling it is to be in physical pain or discomfort and anticipating that could be nerve wracking, such as the anticipation of the pain of going to the dentist and getting your teeth drilled. The anticipation or fear of emotional pain, however, is usually based on the pain of the wounding of self-identity, loss of self-image, lowering of one's status and respect, bruising of ego, or loss of validation. Usually, the higher the status, the bigger the ego and greater the expectation for validation, the easier it is to fall from that high position and for that ego to get more injured. In America, most fears are not about the anticipation of physical pain as most Americans are not usually subjected to physical deprivations or physical attacks (ie., starvation or getting mauled by a lion). Most American fears are about the anticipation of emotional pain (loss of status, the bruising of pride and ego, or losing connection and validation from others). So when two people are bitterly arguing, they're usually attacking each other's egos and diminishing the other person's status (making them "fall" from a higher status to a lower status), and that is what "hurts". It is in losing of status, losing an argument, or being humbled, humiliated, embarrassed, ashamed, excluded or invalidated which is the most the most frightening for most Americans.

However, these kinds of fears and insecurities that most people experience usually aren't actually physically dangerous (ie, an old English saying, "Sticks and stones may break my bones, but words will never hurt me."). Oftentimes, these fears make us overreact, and it's our overreaction which causes more harm than the painful event itself. In this way, these types of fears are very much like some individuals' hyper allergic reaction to a benign substance, such as bee sting venom. For those allergic individuals, getting stung by a bee can be deadly, not because bee sting venom itself will cause deadly harm to the body, but because the body's own immune response is so strong, that it can cause the person's throat to swell, blocking off his airway, which will then suffocate him to death. So it's not the external object itself which is dangerous, but the body's own overreaction to that object which is dangerous.

In a similar way, today, many people's anxieties are extremely over-reactive to even slightly stressful situations. Usually, the stress has to do with losing respect, losing control, or feeling like losing a perceived sense of security. The fear of losing status or respect, fear of rejection, fear of ostracism, or fear of getting left behind, usually these things don't actually do anything to cause real physical harm, but they might bruise our pride, our egos, and our sense of self identity, and the truth is that our pride, our egos and our sense of self identity are really not crucial for our survival. In fact, they may actually be big obstacles for us living happier, more fulfilling, and more faith filled lives.

The concepts of self-identity, self-image, ego, pride, and social status are all man made constructs. As children, we don't have them, but as we get older, as we understand what our expectations are for ourselves. We create our self-identity/self-image based on what our families tell us we should be, what our peers tell us we should be, what our schooling tells us we should be, and what mass media (advertising, fashion, TV, social media, etc.) tells us we should be. As we grow older and start to think with our elevated self-image, and how we "should" be treated, that's when we become more easily hurt when others don't treat us the way we think they should, and the higher or more grandiose the self-image, the harder the fall if someone puts us down or insults us. It's also the reason why when people turn thirty or forty, they might have a little identity crisis because they compare their real lives with what they think they should be. Thus, the pain comes from comparing the successful self-image they have of themselves in their minds with their actual reality, and then feeling like they fall short of it. A big part of the recovery process is to let go of these expectations of where we should be or how much we should have (ie, how successful we are) which we accumulated over our lives, so that we no longer compare ourselves to them and drive ourselves miserable in the process.

With fear being the anticipation of pain, what then is the anticipation of joy or pleasure? I would presume that it's excitement. Many people are afraid of death because either they don't know what's going to happen to them after they die (facing the unknown or losing control), or they're afraid of ending up in eternal torment in hell. However, if people truly believe that they will be in heaven after they die, then there is no more fear of death, as there is no longer an anticipation of the pain of facing the unknown. As Christians, we know that if we confess our sins, truly repent and turn back to God, and believe in Jesus Christ, then we are assured salvation for all eternity and be granted entrance into paradise in heaven. Death no longer becomes something to be frighten of, but instead, becomes something to rejoice.

Scarcity and Abundance

When people no longer feel like they are in a state of scarcity, inadequacy, or poverty that's when they are no longer afraid. They'll no longer have a desire to assert themselves or to dominate over others, to be greedy and hoard everything, to be jealous and want more, or to eliminate what is "threatening" them. It's the feeling of scarcity and inadequacy which causes the fear, and the anticipation of pain. Thus, the opposite of that kind of feeling is to experience great abundance and richness.

The truth is that the experience of scarcity and abundance are never objective. That's why it's possible for a multi-billionaire to still feel like he's poor, whereas a monk with almost no possessions can feel like he's rich.

Feelings of scarcity and abundance are states of mind. A fearful person spends all his thoughts thinking about how much he lacks (based on high expectations), while a calm person thinks about how much great abundance he has (based on humble expectations, being grateful, and acknowledging just how much he's been blessed with every day). The anxious person trains his mind to be more and more anxious by regularly comparing himself with what he expects to have (which is usually a lot, and often, he wants a perfect life), by being ungrateful for what has been given to him, and by thinking about how painful it would be to lose what he already has. Eventually, he becomes really good at being fearful because these scary thoughts of scarcity and inadequacy eventually become habitual and automatic (ie, anything we do repeatedly, we get better at, until those actions become automatic, including finding flaws, inadequacy, and self-criticism). The calm person humbles his expectations and trains his mind until he's grateful for everything in his life, and so, never takes anything for granted. He knows that nothing is permanent, so every sunrise, every person, every meal, and every moment is to be appreciated, because he knows that every day could be his last. He makes a mental habit of being grateful for God's blessings to him, until that habit of gratitude becomes automatic (rather than complaining, or self-criticism).

A humble person also knows that he is not in control of his life, but that ultimately, God is in control of the entire universe. So if it's God's will that today is his last day to be alive, then that's what he has to accept and be grateful for. But the proud person wants to exert control from God and dictate the plan of his own life. The proud person wants to control and predicts everything, assuming his life will go a certain way, his own way, and when things don't go his way, he gets upset. He also often assumes that he's going to live forever, and in the meantime, he doesn't appreciate what he has, until he loses them from his life. Oftentimes, this person will neglect and lose the most important things in his life (his health, his family and friends) in order to purse things that are actually inconsequential (money, status and ego).

I think our society actually has gotten really good at constantly reminding us of how much we lack and to be self-ambitious and to want more, every day. This occurs in families, in school, in business, in advertising, in TV and movies, in social media, and in our expectations and comparisons between us with each other. Every day, we're bombarded by external messages in our lives that cause us to feel inadequate or lacking in something or another. With enough repetition, these thoughts and feelings become automatic and subconscious. The feelings of scarcity and inadequacy eventually become who we are, imbedded deep in our hearts. However, the truth is that we are often blind to just how much we've been blessed with because of our self-ambitious, anxious, and perpetually dissatisfied state of mind. Based on what we see every day, the more expectations we have of everything in our lives to be perfect and instantaneous, the more flaws, the more shortcomings, and the more failures we'll think there are. That's why it's so important to let go of those kinds of expectations of what "perfection" and "success" are supposed to look like that we accumulate from our society, and instead, look to God.

As followers of Christ, we aren't supposed to focus so much of our lives on uplifting our pride, our egos or our self-identity. We are supposed to empty ourselves and diminish our egos so that we don't center our lives on exalting, glorifying, praising and worshipping ourselves.

(Matthew 23:12 "Whoever exalts himself shall be humbled; and whoever humbles himself shall be exalted"). Instead we're supposed to center our lives on exalting, glorifying, praising and worshipping God, and accept that He is always in control of our lives, not us. Thus, when we focus on worshipping, glorifying, and praising God (rather than worshipping, glorifying, and praising our own self-image), then the pain of being insulted, rejected, bullied, and neglected is greatly diminished, and when the pain is diminished, so is the fear. Christians are supposed to focus all of our thoughts, our behaviors, and our actions towards honoring God, not on honoring ourselves, because when we try so hard at on honoring ourselves (or trying to get others to honor us and praise us), and we don't get it (or worse, if someone actually DISHONORS us), then we feel tremendous pain from that fall in status (when we expect glory, but instead, get disrespect).

However, if we only think of ourselves merely as penitent slaves to God, grateful to Him for every moment of every day, and we are empty of pride, ego and the desire for self-image worship and glorification, and our only desire is to glorify, worship, exalt and praise God, then any insult or attack on us as individuals will have no power. Since there's no longer an ego, there's nothing to attack and nothing to injure. As servants of God, this is how we're supposed to be. Fearless to personal attacks because personal attacks are attacks on the ego, on pride, and on the sense of self, and Christians are supposed to be devoid of ego, devoid of pride, and to die to the self.

In my own life, I was the most anxious and most depressed when I felt like my life didn't measure up to what I was supposed to be, what I was supposed to have, and what I was supposed to have accomplished. But looking back, I was a very proud and ambitious person. I wanted my life to be perfect, just like what I saw on TV. I didn't want an ordinary life, or even worse, a low class (poor) life. My greatest fear in life was to end up dirty, broke, homeless, and having to beg for money. My goal was to be rich, successful, powerful, and attractive. I wanted to get to the top, to be in charge, and to be a "big" person. However, if my real life didn't measure up to what I thought I was supposed to be, or things weren't happening the way I thought they were supposed to happen, then that's when my stress and anxiety would increase, and frustration would build, which might lead to anger, addictive behaviors (like binge watching TV), or avoidance of the thing which was causing me to feel stressed.

It was only after I started to make a regular habit of always thanking God for everything in my life that I started to see just how much great abundance I've been blessed with. And with that eye opening experience, my stress level started to drop. I started to focus on how much I truly have, rather than focusing on how much I lacked. I used to focus all my thoughts on how things didn't measure up in my life, how others didn't measure up, and how life didn't measure up. Eventually, with enough practice and repetition, I became really good at complaining, and pointing out flaws, failures, mistakes, and shortcomings. I now realize that feelings of scarcity and the feelings of abundance are states of mind rather than objective external circumstances.

By regularly practicing humility and gratitude towards God's abundance, I became much more relaxed, much more at peace, and I was able to live in and enjoy every moment, rather than constantly upset about things not measuring up from the past, or worrying about things not measuring up in the future. Every day, I would get down on my hands and knees in prayer to thank God for all that he has blessed me with, and throughout the day, I would constantly thank Him, so that whenever I ate, whenever I showered, whenever I put on clothing, whenever I drove, whenever I looked at the beautiful sky, I would always be aware of just how rich, and how blessed, I truly am. I purposely decided not to expose myself to things that would make me compare myself to people with perfect lives. Instead, I chose to always be grateful to God for all that I have, and I'm now a lot more content with my life than ever before.

I realized now just how much our entire society actually wants us to focus on being self-ambitious, self-assertive, competitive, domineering, controlling, conquering, self-glorifying, self-exalting, and self-praising. Parents tell their children that ambition is a virtue and to reach for the stars, advertising tells us to stand out, assert ourselves and to keep up with fashion trends, schools and businesses tell us that the only way to succeed and get ahead is by competing with our peers and by promoting and glorifying ourselves, while denigrating and stepping over our rivals. TV shows, movies, sports, video games, social media, politics and even online pornography all have an element of ego boosting and fantasies of "winning" or "dominating" over others. Boosting the ego is a really big part of our popular "entertainment". Our whole cultural system seems to be based on creating dissatisfied individuals with selfish ambitions and big egos who want more and more and more, rather creating humble and grateful individuals who are happy with what we have, to be generous, and to do good and work hard with our great abundance. Our culture's primary goal seems to be for every individual to feel inadequate and insecure, to want to dominate over others and to be praised and worshipped, rather than to submit to God, glorify, praise, thank and worship Him.

In the United States now, in spite of all the problems we face, we still live in the most abundant and the richest time in all of world history. We can do things and buy things today that people from one hundred years ago and people in other parts of the world would never even dream of. We can fly around the world, live and work in comfortable air conditioned and heated buildings, have endless supply of clean drinkable running water, flush toilets that automatically take away our waste, healthcare that's been able to extend our lives by decades, plenty of abundant and rich foods, an oversupply of warm clothing, cars that allow us to travel at speeds and distances unheard of one hundred years ago, and so much more, yet so most of us don't see all of these blessings because our ambitions, expectations and elevated self-images of ourselves. Compared to other countries and to most prior periods of human history, most Americans live like kings of the past. Yet we only see flaws, inadequacies and scarcity in our lives, rather than the great abundance all around us. For many people, due to our high expectations, all we think about all day long is what we're lacking; money, time, energy, freedom, patience, power, status, respect, etc., until that state of scarcity becomes their entire reality. In this way, abundantly blessed people can still feel poor, due to how they think about their lives in comparison to their expectations. We have so much, and yet, we still feel like we don't have enough. It's like a morbidly obese person who feels like he's experiencing starvation, every moment of every day, even though he's already overfed and overweight. And what's worse is that when people only focus on what they don't have, they feel powerless and hopeless, rather than see just how much they're blessed with, and use that to the best of their ability to do good work.

I honestly think this is the greatest delusion of our culture today. When it comes to being happy and healthy, there are so many people that think that they don't have enough and that they are not enough, when in fact, they have far more than they need, and they are far more than enough. **When we regularly make it a habit of thinking to ourselves just how much scarcity is in our lives, just how much inadequacy we have, and just how much we lack, these kinds of thoughts become automatic and subconscious.** Eventually, these thoughts will start to get more and more easily triggered until they start appearing in our minds automatically. Whatever we do repetitively becomes easier and easier (just like everything else in life, such as learning a new skill, playing a sport, playing an instrument, driving a car, or learning a new language), and that also includes our thought patterns, both good and bad. For most Americans, thoughts of not being good enough, not having enough, not achieving enough, and not getting enough attention has numbered in the millions throughout one's lifetime. Like a muscle that gets overuse, these negative thoughts have a way of getting more and more easily triggered until like a boxer with enough training, they become reflexes, triggered at the slightest provocation.

That's why every day, I pray a simple prayer of gratitude and thanks to God, over and over again, throughout my day, every day. In this way, being humble, grateful, thankful becomes habitual and automatic, instead of thoughts of about scarcity, inadequacy, deficiency, and poverty. Every moment of every day, as often as I can, I repeat the prayer, "Thank You Lord" in my thoughts. With this prayer, I'm made aware of just how abundant and rich my life really is, and has always been. I'm made to acknowledge that everything I experience, everything I am, everything I have, everything I own, everything that I can do, and everyone that I love are wonderful blessings from God. This is very different than how I used to live where all day long, I would ruminate about how much my life fell short of my ideal self-image, or how I didn't measure up to what others have, or how I didn't measure up to my own perfect expectations. This kind of self-criticism, through overuse like an overgrown muscle, became habitual and eventually, an automatic pattern until the thoughts of worthlessness, uselessness, insignificance, failure and not belonging anywhere became extremely strong, very rapid and very constant.

And with such thoughts of scarcity, also came feelings of anxiety, stress, fear, and even hostility. This pattern of focusing so much on my own scarcity and inadequacy made me a very selfish and self-centered person. My whole life was about trying to fulfill my own endless need for more, and more and more, not in thinking about how I can share or contribute to the lives of others.

However, when I started to make it a constant daily practice of thanking God for all I've been blessed with (my health, my safety, my education, my capabilities, my family, my friends, my body, my food, my clothes, my shelter, my car, my job, my life experiences, my money....just too many to count) and acknowledging just how much He has blessed me with, it made me realize just how rich and abundant my life truly is, and I became much more calm and relaxed. Realizing just how full my life is, I also became more generous in giving my time, effort, and resources to others who I thought needed it more than I did, because I was now functioning from a state of abundance rather than a state of scarcity. I no longer focused my attention on how much I lacked, but instead, I focused on how much I truly have and on how much some other people needed more help than I did, and, out of my abundance, how I could fulfill their needs with that abundance.

The Link Between Humility and Love

In my life, there were many times when I didn't like the person I was. I looked at others and I thought to myself, "Why aren't I more like them? I want what they have, not what I have!" Or I would compare myself to perfection and only set my sights up high, and look at my current situation with disdain and contempt. I read novels, watched a lot of TV and movies, and fantasied about how my life "should be" to escape, rather than appreciate my life as it was. It got so bad that eventually, all I could do was to love and appreciate the lives of others, while hating and feeling contempt for my own life and what I had. In this way, it's so easy to want to neglect myself, or even worse, to destroy myself.

I see this pattern, not just in me, but in others around me as well, people who don't appreciate what they have, but instead, are constantly looking at others, constantly looking outside of themselves for happiness, constantly focusing on the next goal, the next step, the next achievement, but never being happy, even after they arrive at their goals. The contentment they seek is always elsewhere, because they never learned to appreciate and be grateful for what they've already been blessed with. We've all been taught in our culture to be ambitious and to want more and more and more; never to settle for mediocrity, never to settle for "just enough". But in the meantime, while we set our eyes on our neighbor's house, our own house often gets neglected and abused.

I see this not only in people who suffer from Depression, but also in neighborhoods where people seem to have given up hope. I've lived in the Oakland Hills for many years, but when I drive through the rough parts of Oakland, I see trash in the streets, graffiti on buildings, liquor stores everywhere, prostitutes, and drugs being sold and used. When I see this, it makes me sad, because it seems like these people don't know how to love their neighborhood. They don't know how to see their streets as valuable, to see their communities as wonderful, to see their people to be cherished, to see their families to be loved and cared for. I don't know why there's so much neglect and lack of care in those neighborhoods, but I know from personal experience with Depression that when I thought my life was worthless and meaningless, it was a struggle just to get through each day.

And that's why it's so important to see what we're been blessed with and what we've received as valuable and wonderful. Instead of setting our sights on what we don't have, and valuing only things that we lack, it's important to humble expectations and see what we **DO** have and value all the things that we have. In this way, we can go from hating what we have and who we are, to loving what we have and who we are. God has blessed us with so much every day, and He wants us to use what we have towards doing His will and to glorify Him. I don't think it pleases Him when we constantly complain to Him about how He hasn't given us enough in our lives. When it comes to lack of gratitude, I think this is one of Adam and Eve's cardinal sins. When they decided that being given paradise wasn't enough, and they wanted to eat from the

Tree of Knowledge of Good and Evil, so that they, in turn, could become "like God".

How Much is Really in the Glass?

Is the glass half full or half empty? It really depends on your perspective. If you look at the glass from the top down, it always looks half empty, and the bigger you make yourself, the more ambitious you set your expectations, the smaller and smaller the glass (and its contents) will seem, until you barely see the glass at all. However, if you look at the glass from the bottom up, it'll always look half full. And the smaller and smaller you make yourself, the bigger and bigger the glass (and its contents) will seem. In this way, scarcity and abundance are based on how ambitious (or proud) versus how humble we choose to be. As Christians, God calls us to be humble and grateful, not proud and ungrateful.

Depending on our perspective, we can see the world as filled with great abundance everywhere, or we can see the world as a desolate landscape, devoid of anything worthwhile.

Chapter 7. The Dangers of Self Idolatry

The concept of idolatry is when people worship anything or anyone other than God. It's when anything takes the place of God in our lives as the focus of our worship and praise. The term came about when the early Israelites in the Bible had a bad habit of worshipping man made things (objects like the golden calf, carved statues, figurines, mountains and trees, and other nation's gods), rather than God Himself. This, of course, was considered a huge sin in the eyes of God, since the people of Israel were supposed to humble themselves, bow down, worship, praise and obey God and God alone. The first two of the Ten Commandments were about worshipping God and to not worship idols. (Exodus 20:2-4) 2 *"I am the Lord your God, who brought you out of Egypt, out of the land of slavery.* 3 *"You shall have no other gods before me.* 4 *"You shall not make for yourself an image in the form of* *anything in heaven above or on the earth beneath or in the waters below."* The worship of idols caused the Israelites to forsake God, and God's instructions for his people (ie, loving God, loving their neighbors, and not doing harm, abusing one another, oppression or callous neglect to their follow Israelites, etc.).

When we worship something, we bow down, uplift and submit to it. We praise it, we glorify it, we exalt it, we obey it and we depend on it. In effect, we become enslaved to it, obeying its will and even sacrificing ourselves and even forsaking our loved ones, just to appease it. Idols could be anything. Idols could be physical objects, they could be money, they could be our jobs, they could be our social ranking, they could be our youth and our beauty, they could be our parents or our loved ones, they could be our marriages, they could be our education levels, or they could be drugs and alcohol. Idols are things that people hold onto for security, for comfort, for a sense of value or purpose, for status, and for relief. Idols are things that people hold onto so that if they lost them, they would no longer feel like their lives are secure, meaningful, fulfilling and worthwhile anymore.

Looking back on my own life, I think about the times that I became depressed and even times when I was thought about suicide. These were times when I felt a great sense of loss of something crucially valuable in my life. The first time was when I was in seventh grade, and I wanted to get perfect grades in order to please my parents, but I couldn't because I nearly flunked a World History test. What I really wanted, which was to get straight A's that semester, but unfortunately, the idea of getting perfect grades was now gone because of the poor results of that test. I would now be a "bad" student, not a "successful" one. My self-image of a "successful" or perfect student was shattered when I realized that my real performance didn't measure up to that expectation. Another time when I was deeply depressed was when I dropped out of graduate school in my mid-twenties. I was really depressed because I felt like a failure, and I felt worthless because of having a tarnished and imperfect image of myself. Again, the perfect and "successful" self - image I had was no longer matching the reality of my life, and that was a person who was now a graduate school dropout, and who was also unemployed and living with his parents. The last time that I was really depressed and even suicidal was when I received the sign from God that eventually led me to write this book. I was in my mid-thirties, I had been working at a good company, making a good salary, and dating a successful and attractive woman whom I thought I was going to soon marry and start a family with. I thought that my life was going on a wonderful path. To me, I was finally going to get "back on track" and have a "successful" life. I was going to have a house, and then purchase additional houses as investment property, be married to a successful woman and have a good career in a successful company. However, all that suddenly fell apart when I was let go from my job, and then soon after, my relationship ended, and I was back to being unemployed, single, and living with my parents. Again, the reality of my life was not even close to matching the "successful" self-image that I had idolized, worshipped, exalted, glorified and wanted praise for.

Throughout my life, my idols have been my parents and other people that I looked up to (when I was a child), my education level (the status of my grades and my schooling), women in my life whom I had relationships with and idolized, my jobs, my physical appearance, and most of all, **the biggest idol I've had in my entire life...has**

been my own "successful" self-image. That "successful" self-image is something inside my mind, a perfect version of myself, which I imagine that I'm supposed to be. In each of the three examples above, when I thought I was going to get imperfect grades in seventh grade, when I thought I was going to have an imperfect self-image because I dropped out of graduate school and was unemployed and living with my parents, and when I lost my job and lost my successful relationship, what hurt me the most was that what I had lost was my "successful" self-image of myself. In a deep part of my mind, I held onto the image of myself working, making lots of money, being successful at my job, handsome, youthful and physically attractive, owning a big house, married to a beautiful wife, raising several wonderful and talented children, and gradually and steadily moving up in society with more money, more assets, and more success in my life and the lives of those I know. In each of these three examples where I became depressed and hated my own life and wanted it to end, I made a comparison between my real life and the life/self-image that I had worshipped and wanted to glorify, and they didn't match at all, that's when I didn't feel like my life was worth living anymore.

Somehow, based on how I was socialized by my upbringing and by my society, my mind has always had a self-image of myself that's been successful, good looking, intelligent, capable, victorious, talented, strong, on top of things, in control, and is able to attract and have sex with young beautiful women. I suppose you can also call this having a lot of pride, being very arrogant, or having a big ego, but this is the reality of who I was. I had an image of myself that I wanted to be glorified, exalted, praised, and maybe even to be worshipped. I wanted this from others, and I wanted this from myself as well. When this didn't happen, when others didn't glorify, exalt, praise and worship me, I got upset. And when I was in a place in my life when I couldn't even do those things for myself (because of my failures and my setbacks in my life), then I got depressed. **When my self-image of myself got so bad that my evaluation of the reality of my situation didn't match at all with where I thought I should be, then I started to really hate my own life, hate my own body, and wanted to end my own life.**

This is why self-idolatry is so dangerous. This is why it's so dangerous to worship one's own self-image and seek praise, exaltation, glory and worship from oneself and others. When we dedicate our entire lives to worshipping our own self-image, not only is it unbiblical in that we are taking away our focus of dedication, worship and praise away from its rightful recipient, that is, away from God, but it also puts tremendous stress on ourselves to work so hard to elevate ourselves so that we would get that adoration and that recognition from others. We might even have to fight and compete with others in order to get this kind of attention, praise, and glorification; sometimes even denigrating others (through bullying, gossip and slander) in order to better glorify and exalt ourselves. Even if we are to build ourselves up, and sit at the top, and be the "successful" person that we've always wanted to be, then we're afraid to lose that status somehow when something changes, and then we become constantly fearful of falling from our high status, down to a lower one.

In addition, this kind of elevation, adoration, and recognition is never entirely in our control, as the act of elevating, adoring, and recognizing us is almost always at the control of others around us. Thus, when circumstances outside of our control occurs, and we lose a job, lose our beauty, lose our health, lose our home, lose our wealth, lose our status, lose our marriage, lose our family members, or lose our children, then that self-image becomes tarnished and the thing that we had spent our entire lives trying to worship, praise and exalt disappears. So now, the thing that we looked to for comfort, security, meaning, and fulfillment in our lives is now gone, and life no longer has any more meaning, and even suicide starts to become more attractive as a way to escape from the pain of not living up to what we think we should be.

However, it doesn't even have to be as bad as being led down a path towards self-destruction. When we dedicate our entire lives and all of our energy towards uplifting and trying to glorify our own self-image, we often become a lot more sensitive, defensive and upset when that self-image is damaged by criticism, by insults, and by comparison to others who might have a better image than us. Therefore, when live our whole lives wanting others to praise and glorify us, and that doesn't happen because we feel neglected, insulted, criticized, overlooked, or even bullied, then, even though our reaction may not turn us towards suicide, it can still lead us towards feeling dissatisfied and offended when we think that others aren't treating us with enough "dignity" and "respect".

Humility and Courage

I think there's a strong link between humility and courage, and on the flip side, between pride and cowardice. When we empty ourselves of our egos, then there is much less for others to attack and wound. So much of what hurts us is when we want to be treated with a certain amount of respect, dignity, or higher status, and when we're treated in a way that is not so respectful, dignified or of a certain high status, then we feel offended because our pride gets hurt. The higher up we try to climb, the more dangerous the fall all the way down to the floor, but when we keep our feet firmly planted on the ground (whether going up or down), then we're always safe, secure, and without anxiety, because we know that we won't have a great distance to fall. The bigger the ego, the higher we want our social standing to be, the more perfect we try to project our lives to others, the more insecure we are to be humbled, humiliated, and insulted. However, if we keep a humble heart all the time, then regardless of how others might try to humble, humiliate or insult us, then we can easily laugh off the attacks as nothing more than silly fun and games.

I think about how the early Christians were persecuted, and how they were insulted, humiliated, denigrated, beaten, tortured, and even killed for holding onto their faith in Christ, I wonder how they were able to endure such abuse. Did they feel emotionally hurt to have been treated like criminals, to see their names get dragged through the mud, to have their reputation be publicly destroyed? Or was their desire towards worshipping, praising and glorifying God so strong that they didn't care any longer about their own reputation and even their own bodies getting destroyed, as long as they were able to exalt and praise the name of God. In the process of letting go of their egos, letting them die to themselves, I think they were able to be in a state of mind where they didn't care whether others exalted and praised them, or whether others denigrated or humiliated them. All they cared about was whether Jesus was glorified, and whether God was exalted and praised, not they themselves.

And when we turn that exaltation, praise, glorification and worship towards God, rather than our own self-image, then we can be happy no matter what our circumstances are in life. When we regularly bow down and praise and thank God for giving us life, for giving us peace, for giving us comfort, for giving us the Bible, for giving us health, for giving us safety, for giving us his son Jesus Christ who died to save us, for giving us money, for giving us shelter, for giving us family, for giving us friends, for giving us the church, etc., then we start to open our eyes to just how abundantly God blesses us with every moment of every day. So much of what causes so many Americans to be upset today is not that we are truly poor or truly lacking in security and in material possessions. What makes us upset is that we PERCEIVE that we're lacking in security and in material possessions.

In America, if you ask almost anybody if they have enough food to eat, enough clothing to keep them warm, or enough shelter to protect them from the elements, almost everyone would say "yes" to all three. **However, what often makes people unhappy is that they still perceive that they don't have an adequate supply of something else that we think is essential for their survival and happiness and they may think that we don't have enough status, not enough respect, not enough popularity, not enough control, not enough power, not enough conquests, not enough security, or not enough success**. It is often this expectation that our lives are supposed to look like the people on TV, in the movies, in magazines, or on social media and when we're told by our peers, by our families, and by our society that we're supposed to look like, how much we're supposed to have, how much we're supposed to achieve, and when we compare our real lives with those models of success and perfection, that's when we become unhappy, because it's then that we realize the reality of our lives don't measure up to the internalized ideal of our self-image, and we are dissatisfied with ourselves. This is why it's so important not to be influenced by the wrong kind of media and the wrong kind of people. By being influenced by these media sources and those kinds of people, we come to believe that our whole lives should be dedicated towards projecting a certain kind of "successful" self-image to the world, one that ultimately, is very unhealthy for us. At best, if our real lives come close to our perfected successful self-images we have of ourselves, we'll be momentarily satisfied with our lives, but we'll still always worry about losing the things, the titles, and the status we've acquired. At worst, if our real lives completely mismatches the successful and perfected self-images we have of ourselves in our minds, then our very lives will be at risk, as we evaluate our lives as useless, worthless and insignificant and we start to hate ourselves in the process.

This is when people become so depressed, and they hate their lives to such an extreme degree that they would rather end their own lives, rather than continue living lives that they feel are worthless and useless. For some people, suicide is quick, but for others, the path of self-destruction lies in addictive escapist self-harming and relationship-harming behaviors such as drug and alcohol abuse, smoking, gambling, sex addition, food addiction, binge watching TV, uncontrolled rage and anger, and even work addiction.

Chapter 8. More on Relieving Fear, Stress and Anxiety

Laughter

There are a few more ways that I've found which helps to reduce stress and tension. One is through laughter. As a child, I didn't laugh very often in my household. None of my relatives laughed very much. However, when I found out about Laughter Yoga, a technique where individuals get together to practice laughter for about an hour, as a form of cardio vascular exercise, I discovered the health benefits of incorporating more laughter into my life. Some people laugh very infrequently, while others laugh all the time. The ones who laugh more regularly seem to have less stress and anxiety, and they also seem to be healthier too (according to the medical doctor who started laughter yoga). As I started practicing more exaggerated laughter every day (mostly in my car, by myself, while listening to comedians), I noticed that my tension level decreased and my confidence level increased. One of the main premises behind laughter yoga is that our bodies can't differentiate between real laughter and fake laughter. You still get the same health benefits and stress relief benefits whether the laughter is real or fake. Therefore, they encourage fake laughter, until it becomes real laughter. It might be awkward at first, and you might feel silly or even "crazy", but eventually, the body becomes trained to laugh more easily and more reflexively. Discharging stress and tension through laughter is far better and less frightening than discharging stress through yelling and screaming, something which many people also do (unfortunately), at the expense of those around them. Being humble and able to laugh at one's self is so important for discharging stress and tension, but it takes practice. Some people like to laugh at others, but this could sometimes become bullying or hurtful behavior, while being able to make fun of and laugh at one's self is always safe and shows a level of self-confidence and courage.

Retraining the Mind for Positive Self Talk

Another method I've discovered is the use of positive self-affirmations several hundreds or even several thousands of times a day. This is to counteract the negative self-criticism that most people experience every day. In our culture, it's very easy to have negative self-talk (ie, "you're no good", "you're a failure", "you're an idiot", "you're ugly", "you're stupid", "you don't belong here", etc.) We might repeat these thoughts to ourselves over and over again, and the problem is that whatever the human body does repeatedly, it gets better and better at it. Therefore, even self-criticism is something that many people may not realize they're training themselves to do, every time they repeat a self-critical thought. Therefore, by training the mind to have positive self-affirmations several hundred times a day, the mind is inoculating itself against the self-criticism which can easily occur when we compare ourselves with others, when we feel like we don't measure up, or when we are frustrated with ourselves over something. We may not realize it, but even our thoughts are often automatic, and the more negative thoughts we have, the more those kinds of thoughts appear in our minds. So telling ourselves positive things like, "It's going to be ok", "You're a good person", "You're valuable", "You're useful", "You belong here", "You're capable", "You're responsible", "You're productive", "You're intelligent", "You're courageous", hundreds or thousands of times a day will eventually embed these thoughts into the mind, and these thoughts will eventually become reflexive, much like a boxer's reactions through tens of thousands of repeated patterned movements. A boxer doesn't even have to think about how to react, he just does, and a person who's trained himself to have positive affirmations has the same kinds of reflexes (as does a person who trains himself to have negative self-talk as well, unfortunately). The only problem is that this type of training could create very inflated self-esteem and self-confidence, to the point of arrogance. This is why I now repeat the thought "Thank you Lord" as a way of humbling myself to God, and reminding myself that everything I have comes from God.

Inducing Healthy Pain/Discomfort to Alleviate the Anticipation of Pain

Another method of alleviating fear and stress is by inducing a little bit of healthy pain/discomfort. This could be through exercise, stretching, taking cold showers (gradually lowering the temperature of showers), periodic fasting, and even eating spicy foods. The premise of these strategies is that they're painful, or at least, uncomfortable (which is why most people avoid doing it). But as I mentioned earlier, fear, stress and anxiety are the anticipation of pain. Therefore, if we're stressed out all day, our bodies are anticipating something painful happening, all day long (whether physical or emotional). Our bodies are preparing us for something negative happening to us, some kind of danger. We're anticipating something uncomfortable, sometimes for weeks, months or even years and years. However, this painful thing usually doesn't happen, and that's where actually experiencing pain comes in to play. If our bodies are anticipating pain, but we're not getting it, then the body is going to continue to anticipate it, without relief, but once we work out our bodies and experience those painful and strenuous exercise periods, then our bodies can finally relax because it's experienced that which it's been anticipating (pain).

The pain and discomfort of these techniques are not actually harmful. In fact, they're really beneficial. There are some people who like to really hurt themselves by cutting or burning their skin. This method of causing pain is similar in that it also alleviates stress by causing the body to experience anticipated pain, however, cutting and burning are much more injurious to the body and can cause scars and infection. Strenuous physical exercise, stretching (like yoga) or eating spicy foods are far more beneficial ways to experience anticipated pain, and stress/anxiety relief than causing oneself physical harm.

Truth-be-told, I think that modern Americans experience less physical pain than ever before. We shield ourselves from physical toil and pain through medication, through modern conveniences like cars, washing machines, tractors and power tools. We try to make sure that we experiences as little physical pain and as much physical comfort as possible. However, this was not the case throughout human history. Humanity has always had physical hardships in the form of farming, washing, cooking, cleaning, working, child birth, etc. Historically, human beings have always experienced some level of physical discomfort throughout our day, and our bodies were probably adapted to expect it, but now, we no longer have such physically uncomfortable experiences, and because of that absence, our minds anticipate pain and discomfort which do not come, and this is one of the factors that cause anxiety and stress. It's the anticipation of pain, which will not arrive.

In my experience, putting my body through some physically strenuous activity, whether exercise or manual labor, not only makes me less anxious and less insecure, but it also makes me more confident and more courageous. I don't think that courage could be achieved without experiencing pain. It's only through experiencing pain, and knowing how to endure it and be tolerant of it that people can face hardship and challenging and awkward situations in life. If we try to protect ourselves, comfort ourselves, or shelter ourselves from painful or uncomfortable situations, then we will always remain insecure, anxious, and even cowardly, and we will never grow. This is what I fear for the younger generation of Americans today, who seem to be so sheltered, so uplifted by their parents and teachers, and so over-protected that they never have to endure any pain, hardship, or awkwardness. So instead of being confident and emotionally resilient, many of them are fragile, insecure, and need everything to be comfortable and perfect for them. Unfortunately, without a dose of healthy pain in their lives, I'm concerned that they will never be the free, brave, and strong citizens that their great-grandparents were who had to endure harsh periods of American history like the Great Depression, and World War II, and the Korean War.

Chapter 9. Conclusion

"Help people overcome fear, but it can only happen through a relationship with God." I can't say it's been an easy journey from the day I heard that message until now. Since that day, I've racked my brain as to how I could do that. There were times that I put myself in that were truly frightening, and which really humbled me. How could I believe in something that I was always taught to dismiss and even ridicule? How could I trust in something that's so ephemeral and lacking in definitive substance, such as God? How could I just let my intuition and my "feelings" take control, rather than my sound, rational, reasonable, logical and analytical mind? What if my intuition and my "feelings" lead me astray? What will happen to me then?

These six years have been hard, filled with ups and downs, successes and failures, but I believe now that through it all, God has always been with me, giving me direction when He felt like I needed it, giving me clues and hints in order to guide me and protect me from serious harm. And times when I did struggle when I wanted to give up and just live a "normal" life, those times were always meant to strengthen me, to embolden me, to discipline me, to humble me, to make me wiser and to be more reliant on God. Now, no matter what, I've learned to be always grateful and content with what God has provided me.

I humbly bow down to God every day, and I thank Him non-stop in my thoughts and in my prayers. I remind myself that I'm not the center of the universe, that I'm not supposed to the one to be glorified, exalted, and praised but that it's God that I need to glorify, exalt, and praise. I remind myself that I don't know everything, and that I have to know my place in the universe, which is extremely small and limited in nature. My whole life, I wanted to worship and uplift my own self-image, and it's caused me so much stress, pain, and even hopelessness at times. Now, I dedicate my life towards exalting and glorifying God, and I'm so much more at peace than ever before.

I finally realize now that my life isn't about me anymore. It's not about how successful, popular, famous, attractive, capable, righteous, generous, or how high up I can climb over others. No, my life is now directed at how popular, famous, attractive, righteous, generous and how high up **GOD** can climb. As a Christian, I'm supposed to "Love God and Love my Neighbor". For most of the time that I called myself Christian, I wasn't even sure if God existed, so it was really hard for me to love Him, and faithfully, be obedient to His will. Now that I know that it's always been my own pride, ego, arrogance, self-glorifying and self-worshipping idolatrous nature that has been preventing me from bowing down, humbling myself before God, before Jesus, and before the Bible.

I think there was a reason why the first four of the Ten Commandments have always been about honoring, worshipping and loving God, while the next six were about how to love one another. From the beginning, we were always supposed to have revered God above all else. We were always supposed to have taken Him seriously, and not just thought of Him as an accessory, or limit His role and His power in our lives, but in my pride, arrogance and defiance, I didn't understand how important it was to worship and praise God. Now, I finally understand and that's why I wanted to write this book so that I can share it with others who might also be struggling with their faith, and who also want to live a happier, more content, and more abundant lives, glorifying and exalting God first above all else, even though our society and our culture may tell us to do otherwise.

When I received my sign in 2012 to help people overcome fear through a relationship with God, I was a very anxious person, very frightened, very stressed out, and very mistrustful of everyone and everything. My mind anticipated pain from everywhere and everyone all the time. I was always nervous, thinking that I was always going to get hurt. I tried to project a perfect image of myself to the world, but actually feeling really scared and vulnerable inside. I would easily lose my temper and become frustrated with even the smallest things. I used TV, movies, pornography, and social media as ways of distracting and numbing myself from my fears and worries. However, these past six years in which God has guided my life, in which God has protected and reassured me, in which God has calmed me down, and soothed my fears and taken away my pain and my trauma, I can tell that there is something very different about my mind and my heart. I can tell that I'm no longer as easily agitated as I used to be. I can tell that I don't lose my temper nearly as easily as I used to. I can tell that I don't overreact to situations like I used to. I can feel the difference in my mind and in my heart. There's a new calm and peace that I now have which God has given me. I now know that no matter what happens in my life, and even in my death, that I will be all right because God is with me and that God will always be with me for all eternity in paradise, after I die. When people disrespect me, when people insult me, when people treat me unfairly, when people look down on me, when people humiliate me, when people ignore me, when people abandon me, these things just don't bother me as much as they used to. It still hurts when they happen, but not as much as before because I know that God gives me strength, that God gives me comfort, that God heals my wounds, and God restores my soul. I know that God is always in control, and I trust in Him in always. I wish others can also experience that peace and that tranquility, especially members of my own family who are still struggling.

Thank you so much for reading this book, and for allowing me to share my walk with God with you. I hope that it's made you think a little bit about how important it is to look to always look to and to rely on Him, rather than to rely on ourselves, and how dangerous it is to base our lives on promoting our own self-image. I know it's taken me a long time to learn this, and it almost cost me my life, but God was there to save me and I truly believe now that God wastes nothing, not even painful experiences like suffering and despair, because without such experiences, we wouldn't know just how much we need truly God in our lives. Take care, and I wish you peace, and abundant blessings.

About the Author

Tony Koo is a devout Christian who lives in the San Francisco Bay Area. He went to UCLA and got his degree in Business Economics in 1997, but his current passions lie in psychology and spirituality, especially after he received his life-saving calling from God to help others overcome fear, in 2012. He loves people, and is currently semi-retired, driving part -time for Lyft (a smartphone based ride sharing company) to supplement his income, and also to engage with everyday people to hear their stories and to share insights on how to live a happier life. He also actively volunteers at his church, enjoys spending time with his family members, and loves exercising as a way of not only improving physical health, but also to build a tolerance for discomfort, to reduce anxiety and to improve confidence. He hopes to open people's eyes to just how much abundance that God has blessed us with, and to do good things with our abundant blessings. He enjoys meeting different people, traveling to different places, and enjoying good food and beautiful sights.